IMAGES OF ENGLAND

# PAIGNTON
## A CENTURY OF CHANGE

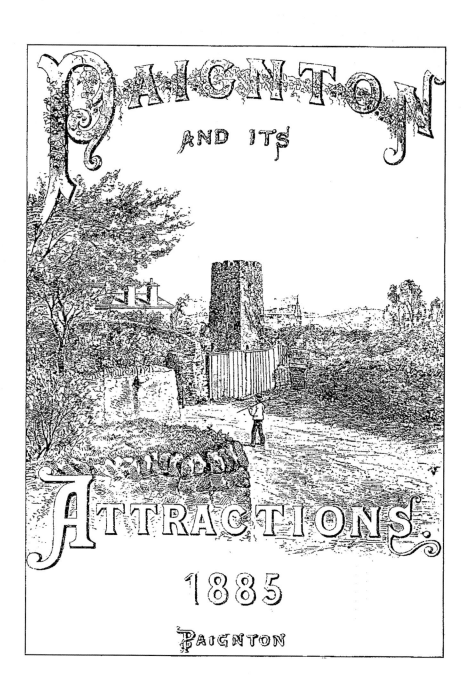

# PAIGNTON

## AND ITS

# ATTRACTIONS

## 1885

### PAIGNTON

IMAGES OF ENGLAND

# PAIGNTON
## A CENTURY OF CHANGE

ALAN HEATHER

The History Press

First published in 2007
Reprinted 2013

The History Press
The Mill, Brimscombe Port,
Stroud, Gloucestershire, GL5 2QG
www.thehistorypress.co.uk

British Library Cataloguing in Publication Data.
A catalogue record for this book is available from the British Library.

ISBN 978 0 7524 4464 2

Typesetting and origination by
The History Press.
Printed and bound in Great Britain by
Marston Book Services Limited, Didcot

# Contents

Paignton seafront and harbour.

# Acknowledgements

I give grateful thanks to my wife Jeanne who never lost her grace, good humour and patience with me during the process of compiling this book.

Also to my family who gave me such wonderful encouragement and support.

Others who have assisted me with pictures and information are: Ray Bond, Clive and Sue Figes, Marygwen Furneaux, Peter Jenkins, Douglas Pulle, the *Herald Express*, Paignton Club, the Redcliffe Hotel, Heather and Tim Reed, Torquay Museum, Torquay Reference Library (in particular librarian Mark Pool) and Colin Vosper. Thank you all.

This book is dedicated to my former co-author David Mason who died just eight weeks after our *Torquay – A Century of Change* appeared in bookshops. I kept a picture of him in front of me while compiling this volume and have tried to achieve the excellent standard he would have expected had he lived.

Care has been taken to avoid using pictures which have been published in a number of previous books containing images of Paignton. They have been kept to a minimum.

Reasonable efforts were made to seek permission from owners of copyright but in the case of old postcards it has often been very difficult.

# Introduction

Paignton is the oldest of the three Tor Bay towns stretching back nearly thirteen centuries when Paega, a religious Saxon leader, arrived here. His small group were looking for a place on which to establish a church and develop some agricultural land. It became known as Paega's tun, an enclosure or village. The Domesday Book lists it as Peinton – the farm tun of Paega's people. Throughout the seventeenth and eighteenth centuries records show it as Paington until in 1833 parish registers referred to it as Paignton.

When I first decided to write this book I knew I would enjoy writing about our local heritage and more importantly about the place where I have lived for many years.

I have spent many fruitful hours obtaining what I believe to be accurate information and presenting the results of my research in a way I hope will be at the same time entertaining and a useful reference book to dip into when required.

It is dedicated to my good friend and co-author David Mason, who was chairman of the Torbay Postcard Club. He unfortunately passed away shortly after our successful *Torquay – A Century of Change* was published last year. He had allowed me to scan pictures from his large collection of postcards and photographs. Now he has gone I arranged with the publisher to compile this book, *Paignton – A Century of Change*, on the understanding I would dedicate it to his memory.

It has been a labour of love, a worthwhile project that has kept me out of mischief doing what I have always loved, creative journalism. I hope it brings other people pleasure, now and in the future.

It is important our heritage here in Paignton is not forgotten and allowed to disappear. There are many references and images of the history of this area but I have tried to focus on the story of Paignton and those who lived here.

Alan Heather
*May 2007*

one

# Holidays

Where is Paignton? It rests on the coast of south Devon at Tor Bay. The bay is semicircular and faces due east. It has at the northern end of its coastline the fashionable upmarket resort of Torquay; the family resort of Paignton in the centre and the fishing port of Brixham at the southern end. The area was always very popular for holidays and favoured for its beautiful scenery, safe beaches and a warm climate.

The arrival of the railway in Paignton in 1859 and the change in May 1892 from Brunel's 7ft broad gauge to the standard gauge meant trains from the Midlands and the North could arrive in the resort.

The first railway station stood alone in the 'Marsh' and was replaced by the present one in 1886. In 1903 the holiday line to the West was first advertised by the Great Western Railway (GWR).

The author believes this photograph of troops in 1914-18 war uniforms pictured here in Queen's Park, with the railway station behind, must be the soldiers who were sent from Paignton to France and Belgium to fight for their country.

ENGLAND AND WALES

G W R

ORDNANCE SURVEY
"ONE-INCH" MAP
Fifth (Relief) Edition

The salubrious air attracted ramblers as this drawing on the front of the 1925 1in/1 mile Ordnance Survey map by artist Ellis Martin shows.

In 1911 the arrival of trams in Paignton caused the demise of the GWR buses. This photo, probably taken with an inexpensive box camera, shows the tight turn trams had to make from Torquay Road into Hyde Road. They were very popular and by 1928 over a million passengers had been carried. The trams were finally replaced early in 1934 with Devon General buses. Although trolley buses were in vogue at the time an attempt to introduce them into Torbay failed.

Later motorcycles had become an affordable mode of transport as depicted on front cover of the Matchless catalogue for 1929. The young lady taking the photograph could clearly not have arrived on this machine!

Ordnance Survey artist Ellis Martin was keeping up with the times with this drawing on the cover of the *Tourist, Popular and District Maps of the 1930s*. It has four sales targets; walkers, cyclists, motorists and trippers. It was the age of new access to the countryside for town dwellers and desk or factory workers.

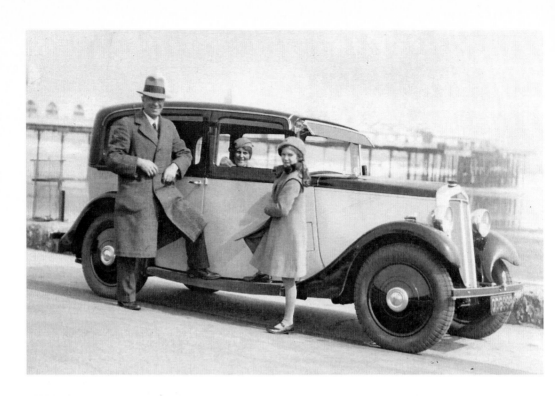

On the left are Dixon's Torbay Luxury Camp and the South Devon Holiday Camp at the top of Smallcombe Road, Foxhole, which, in the 1930s, were owned by C. Swint with J.L. Dixon as the manager. In early 1940 the camps were requisitioned as prisoner-of-war camps until after the fall of France; they were then used as rest camps by the Army's British Expeditionary Force returning from Dunkirk.

*Opposite above:* A family snapshot taken during a visit to Paignton seafront after a wartime ban that made the coast out of bounds was lifted.

*Opposite below:* When the author first arrived at Paignton in May 1959, the holiday season was in full swing. Holiday camps, camping and caravan sites were in abundance. Despite present easy foreign travel to warmer countries, this aerial shot taken in more recent years above the ring road looking towards the bay needs little explanation. How many caravans?

Descending Kings Ash Hill we pass Pontin's Holiday Camp which many people reading this book will remember. It was bought by Mr Fred Pontin. This site was closed in the 1980s. Pontin's (South Devon) Ltd also owned the Torbay Chalet Hotel at Marldon.

*Opposite above:* The Torbay Chalet Hotel which once stood just off the main road near Cox's garage at Marldon with views down across the Westerland valley.

*Opposite below:* Saltern Cove showing the Waterside Camp in the distance. It was started by a group of businessmen in the late 1920s.

SALTERN COVE AND CAMP, PAIGNTON.

The site before the start of the summer season which was purchased by the council in May 1939. It closed at the outbreak of the Second World War and reopened after the war was over. In 1952 main drainage was provided and many improvements were made.

The author's tent is on the headland beyond the railway line and parked alongside is his 1929 beetle-back MG car.

New owners in the 1930s were Mr and Mrs Corney who lived in a detached house at the entrance to the site adjoining Saltern Road. Then it was more a 'camp site' providing tented accommodation and touring caravans.

At the bottom of Kings Ash Hill was The Nest holiday site tucked away in the trees. It was constructed in 1925 and Leslie Boyce was managing director. It was the first holiday camp in Paignton.

*Opposite above:* The Nest was situated on a triangular site between Kings Ash Road, Colley End Road and Foxhole Road and comprised a group of wooden chalets. The site has now been developed for housing in what is now Two Acre Close.

*Opposite below:* Listed as a holiday camp in 1941, Louisville was situated in the Dartmouth Road near Three Beaches.

*Right:* Later the author bought a house on Kings Ash Road and in the field opposite farmer Came was busy turning over the cut grass. In the background Paignton School has been built on the meadow opposite the zoo.

*Below:* And it was not always idyllic as this snapshot taken from the author's back room window in 1967 shows!

Along the main road from Paignton to Totnes was the Ayreville Holiday Camp. Originally it was very primitive as can be seen by these two railway carriages converted into individual chalets, with the loos outside.

This was the well-known entrance to the site.

two

# Along the
# Coast

At Broadsands this pre-war picture shows stooks of corn in the field above the beach. As its name suggests it has broad sands when the tide is out. Cars are parked on an embankment built to protect the marshland behind

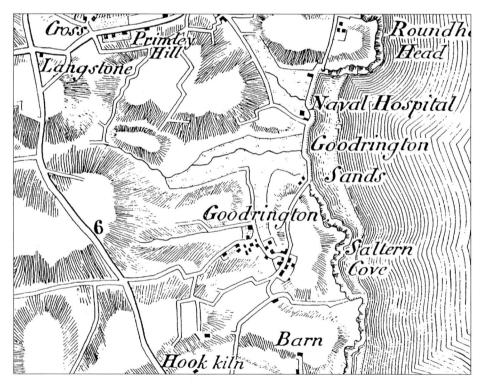

Part of the 1809 map of 'Paington'. During the town's long history there have been as many as thirty variations of its name. Locals' opinions in the Victorian era were divided about the spelling which was finally resolved by the local postmaster who preferred 'Paignton'.

Three Beaches from one of the caravan sites further inland – prominent is the Church of St George.

The church was designed by Edward Maufe, architect of Guildford Cathedral. It was constructed in 1938 by the Harvey family who built many of the fine buildings in Torquay and was consecrated on 25 March 1939. The buildings, proposed to be on the left, were added in the late 1960s and built where they would be more convenient on the right-hand side.

A very rare image of Goodrington which may be the only picture clearly showing Simla in the middle distance on the left. It was the summer home of Charles Pratt Kennedy, a British Army Officer who fought in the Indian Ghurka War and later became a civil servant. He is considered to be the founder of Shimla, formerly Simla, the summer capital of British India and now capital of Himachal Pradesh. Charles died in 1875.

*Opposite above:* An aerial shot taken in the 1920s shows the southern beach and the waterways flowing down from inland and two pipes on the beach letting the surface water flow into the sea.

*Opposite below:* Two pipes which were remnants of Brunel's 'Atmospheric' railway which was abandoned in September 1848. A section of the old piping from the lines was used until recent years on the beach as a surface-water outfall.

Goodrington Beach, Paignton.

Goodrington is situated on a low coastal plain which was poorly drained. There was marshland and a large lake called May's Pool or the Witches' Pool. Parents warned their children of dire consequences if they fell in the 'bottomless pool'. It was later found to be only 2ft deep.

The scene now shows that the land behind the beach was still very marshy and dangerous but a protective sea wall has been built by two local building firms to prevent flooding from rough seas.

Men from the council remove the drying seaweed at low tide when it gives off a pungent and unpleasant smell in the hot sunshine. Behind is Roundham Head and Paradise Point.

Goodrington as we know it today began to emerge in 1929. Funds from the 'distressed arms relief scheme' enabled an army of imported Welsh labourers to start a project to strengthen and beautify Roundham Head.

By 1931 80,000 tons of sandstone had been removed to prevent coastal erosion and a promenade constructed. There were zigzag paths built up the side of the cliff to enable easy access to the headland.

CLIFF GARDENS AND PROMENADE, GOODRINGON, PAIGNTON.

When finished, the beds between the paths were very bare. They looked raw and stark so Herbert Whitley provided many subtropical plants, shrubs and trees to heal the scars and create luxurious surroundings.

The Cliff Gardens and promenade were opened by the Honourable A.V. Alexander in September 1931. They were closed during the Second World War and afterwards were still very popular and enjoyed by visitors and locals alike.

Goodrington beaches were now enjoyed by thousands of people. The children shown here are enjoying a Punch and Judy show.

*Left:* Another event taking place during the annual Children's Week at Goodrington and Paignton was the competition to make the best sandcastle. It was a race against time before the tide came in again and judges arrived to choose the winners.

*Below:* The fancy-dress entrants lined up to have their photograph taken. Were you among them?

*Right:* These people are enjoying
themselves in Young's Park in the 1950s.
The feared May's Pool has long gone
and was made into three lakes: one for
children and adults to use to sail their
model yachts and boats; another for
small motor boats to enjoy; and the third
for the ducks and swans.

*Below:* The hot weather being enjoyed
by families. Here is a cricket match in
progress. No prizes but have some fun
using this picture as a 'spot the ball'
competition.

*Left:* It's goodbye from Goodrington where we have been having a lovely time, we and our donkey friends.

*Below:* Roundham Head is where the Ocean Hotel was once situated. In 1935 the land was laid out in ornamental fashion described by some as, 'a site of verdure, floral and aquatic splendour'. The headland has wonderful views of the whole of Tor Bay.

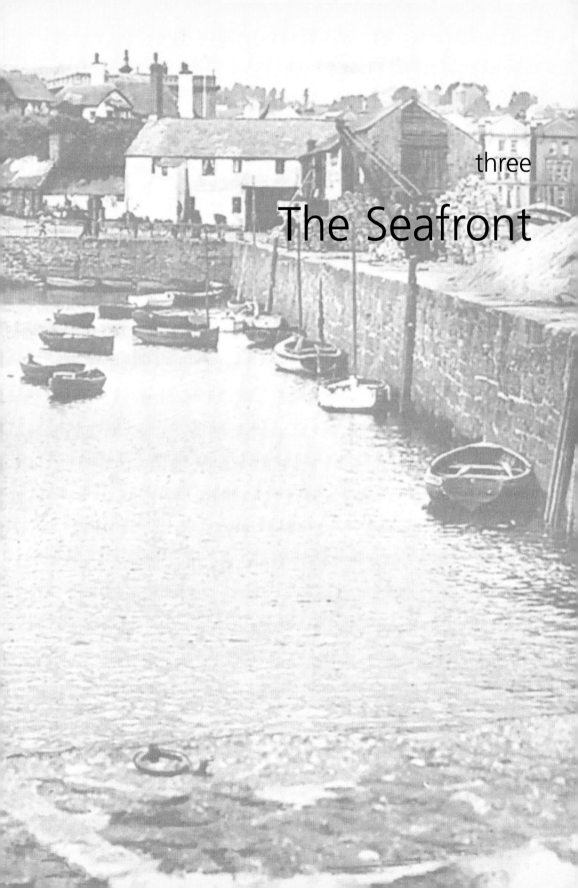

three

# The Seafront

This image of Paignton Harbour was taken during the First World War. The harbour was taken over for a short while by the Royal Navy. A sailor stands at the entrance to the harbour master's office.

This view alongside Roundham Road shows the pavement under construction. The large schooner, which was registered in Plymouth, arrived regularly to deliver coal, culm, timber and cement for building.

Before the return sailing it collected hogsheads of Paignton's famous cider for export. Thousands of gallons were shipped annually to London and Dublin. It also took the legendary Paignton 'flatpole' cabbages to Plymouth from where vast amounts were sold to distant markets.

*Above:* The advent of the railway began to take its toll on the use of the harbour by commercial trading vessels. Later the quay was used for laying out fishing nets to dry.

*Below:* During Paignton Regatta week large crowds watched the sailing races from the harbour walls.

Torbay (Paignton) Sailing Club based at the harbour, held sailing races most weekends when the weather allowed.

Alongside the harbour at the southern end of the Paignton beach was a row of thatched fishermen's cottages which had cellars with direct access to the beach. They were said to have been used to store contraband early in the last century.

*Opposite above:* An aerial view of the harbour entrance emphasising the narrowness of the entrance and how well it protected moored boats.

*Opposite below:* This aerial picture was taken around 1916 and is a lithographic print. It is extremely interesting as it shows how small Paignton was when the photograph was taken. Dating it was difficult but it can be seen that the sea wall at Preston is breached (in February 1915) and Preston Halt railway station buildings are still visible.

PROMENADE & GENTLEMAN'S CLUB, PAIGNTON.

Another early photograph of the building. Mr George S. Bridgman, a clever and well-known architect in the town and Mr Cummins, were asked to draw up plans for the new club house. It was later described in Kelly's *Devon Directory* of 1939 as being, 'in the Classic style relieved in front by six columns supporting a balcony'.

*Opposite above:* The cottages were later demolished and in 1882 a club 'purpose-built for gentlemen' was constructed on the site. The club opened on 22 January 1885 and has remained in use ever since.

*Opposite below:* The club catered for the 'gentry' who had built large villas in the Roundham area. It had all the facilities a social club would need: bar, billiard room, card room and so on. Today it still upholds the standards of good conduct, dress, good fellowship and respect for the rules.

Queen Victoria's Jubilee Year, 1887. A tender of £8 6s was accepted to repaint the woodwork 'provided that Torbay Paint was used', and Mr Langler was asked to provide illuminations outside at the lowest price possible. He charged £19 6s which drew some caustic comments at the next committee meeting.

Fearing a recurrence of the damage caused by the 1824 storm, the Paignton Local Board took over the Green in April 1867 and constructed a sea wall and promenade. This view is from the Gentlemen's Club. In August 1879, a Deed of Gift was signed and the whole of Paignton Green passed into public ownership.

An early summer picture of the promenade with a band playing in a steel shed called the Shelter.

A nice clear promenade along which to stroll and take in the healthy sea air.

Leisure pursuits on Paignton Sands were run privately by Arthur Hyde Dendy. From 1866 regulations forbade men and women swimming together. Mr Dendy's Paignton Bathing Co. later operated the bathing machines and tents. Men had to use Preston beach and the women had to use Paignton beach. Attitudes gradually changed and mixed bathing was eventually allowed.

The bathing company was eventually sold to Paignton Urban District Council in 1921. There were thirty bathing machines and it was proclaimed that the modern bather no longer wanted to be towed down to the waves, 'They may have served some purpose in the Victorian era but now they have no merit of ornament or utility', it was said.

A crowded seafront on the promenade during the annual Paignton Regatta week. The Green is occupied by Hancocks Fair which first arrived in 1900 on the North Green.

The view along Esplanade Road showing all the fairground horse-drawn caravans and vehicles parked neatly on the Green and a large switchback roller coaster.

Hancocks Moving Pictures Show is in progress and fairgoers are patiently and excitingly awaiting the next performance. Adults paid 6d and children paid 3d. In 1920 there was a disastrous fire at Plymouth which destroyed all their equipment and since then a fair has been provided by Anderton and Rowland's.

Paignton beaches for many years were owned by the Duchy of Cornwall which offered them to the Local Board for £220 in 1883. That price was considered too much and it was not until twenty years later that they were acquired for £256.

# Paignton Bathing Company, Ltd.

A LARGE NUMBER OF

## WELL-APPOINTED BATHING MACHINES,

*Fitted with every convenience, and drawn to the water's edge.*

### MALE AND FEMALE ATTENDANTS.

### FINE, FIRM, GENTLY SLOPING SANDS.

## The Safest Bathing Place in the Kingdom.

A bathing advertisement.

The promenade in the 1940s, after the end of the Second World War.

The party having their group photo taken appear to have arrived on a day trip to Paignton. They are all in their best town clothes which we would consider today to be totally unsuitable to wear on the beach. The gentleman in the front with an umbrella looks as though he was the group's leader.

It must be high tide because these donkeys in the 1950s are giving rides on the promenade and not on the beach. Donkeys have always been a very popular traditional attraction at Paignton.

In 1887 a drinking fountain and lamp standard were erected in the centre of the seafront to commemorate Queen Victoria's Golden Jubilee. It was paid for by public subscription. When it was removed it curiously disappeared without anyone knowing where it went. Perhaps a reader will know.

Now we are looking back at the way we have just come. The tide is well out and the bathing cabins for the ladies are left high and dry.

This is another view from the same spot as on the previous page and one of two children on the promenade appear to be buying ice creams from what the author believes might be Mr Pelosi's ice-cream sales cart.

Another view looking back from the Pier.

SOUTH VIEW FROM PIER. PAIGNTON

Pelosi's ice-cream van.

THE KING'S COASTGUARD.

This is a recruitment poster. The coastguard is standing on the southern end of the beach near the harbour.

*Opposite above:* A pleasure boat took people to Torquay, Brixham, Teignmouth and Dartmouth, weather permitting.

*Opposite below:* The Pier looking back towards its entrance.

The beach tents are in two rows, the ones at the front being for the upper classes and those behind for the lower classes.

In February 1915 part of the sea wall at Preston opposite Manor Road was washed away in a storm.

The gap in the wall has never been repaired and can still be seen today.

Starting in May 1919, flights were being offered around the bay. Three Avro seaplanes took two visitors at a time for 25s. They were kept in an elaborate hangar Paris Singer had built on the Green abutting the Redcliffe hotel. The planes taxied along to near Paignton Pier where passengers climbed aboard for their short flights.

Captain Alan Story was one of the pilots helping entertain visitors in this immediate post-war period. Another was Captain Percival Phillips who took this photograph from his Avro 504K aeroplane G-EBIZ whilst flying joy rides.

Pioneer aviator F.P. Raynham is taking off from the beach at Paignton. Another aviator who flew from there was Henri Salmet.

The *Daily Mail* was at the forefront for many years promoting aviation. It brought its famous *Daily Mail* Tour to Paignton in 1912 and again in 1914.

Two rows of tents from the promenade have been moved on to the beach.

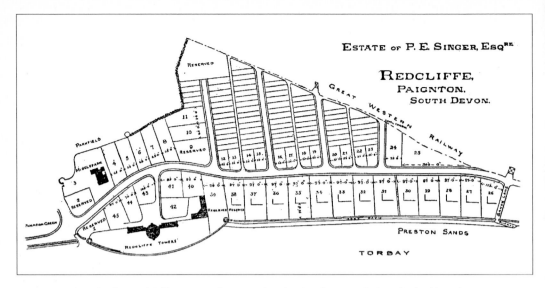

Paris Singer bought the Redcliffe Estate and surrounding land and prepared plans for buildings between the road and sea wall. These were rejected and his dream was never realised.

As owner of Preston Green, during 1911-12, Paris Singer built homes along Marine Drive on the westward side of the Green, protected from the sea's dangers. Here tennis is being played on the Green.

four

# Green and Pier

The entrance to the promenade and the Green from Torbay Road, c. 1905. There are lovely flower beds along the edge of Esplanade Road and parked in the road is one of the early GWR motor buses. On the end of the Pier can be seen the very successful new pavilion.

Taken on Paignton Pier, these healthy and hardy young members of Paignton Amateur Swimming Club participated in the club's opening dip on 20 May 1911.

Disaster struck the Pier on 18 June 1919 when a major fire enveloped the seaward end and destroyed the Pier pavilion. Elegantly decorated, it had been admirably adapted for balls, concerts and all kinds of entertainment. It had a moveable stage. The grand piano was set ablaze and plummeted down into the sea with much of the Pier's structure.

A wooden latticed arch was constructed opposite the bottom of Torbay Road to celebrate the Silver Jubilee of King George V and Queen Mary in 1935. It was illuminated by hundreds of lamps installed by the Paignton Electric Light Co. The arch remained as a tourist attraction until 1936 when the King died. It had then become inappropriate and so it was removed.

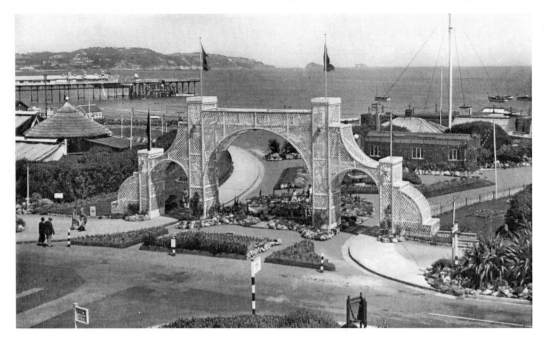

In the post-war years a bandstand was built protected from the weather by a canvas awning and the audience was protected by a much larger one.

REST GARDEN AND PUTTING GREEN, PAIGNTON.

Rest Gardens and Putting Green.

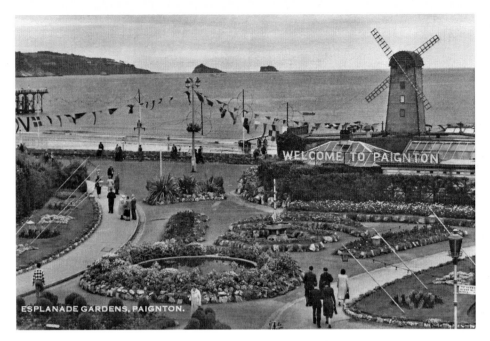

In the 1950s a wood and canvas 'windmill' was erected on top of the entertainments manager's office. The 'Welcome to Paignton' sign was illuminated at night and became a firm favourite with visitors and residents as they approached and arrived at the seafront.

The Green was used for many purposes by local clubs. The Paignton Amateur Athletic Club is holding one of its sports events. Free car parking on the Green was allowed up to 1926. They were then permitted to park at 1s 6d (15p) per day. From 1934 all car parking on the Green was banned.

The diploma which was presented to Mr R. Hole for being first in the 880 yards running event in the Devon County Amateur Athletic Association's Inter-Town Contest held at Paignton in August 1932. It was possibly the same event also pictured.

The Torbay Carnival starts from the promenade at Paignton and this car bedecked with flowers has two judge's award certificates on the windscreen. Behind can be seen one of the many bands that support the carnival procession. Many pounds are raised for various local charities.

The Paignton Hospital sweep float pulled by a Paignton Urban District Council surveyors' department steam-driven flat-bed lorry. There are references to 'Not Ireland, Dora and D.O.R.A.' the author leaves you, the reader, to find out to what they refer.

Prominent in this aerial picture of Paignton Green taken in 1946 shortly after the Second World War is the new large awning to protect the people listening to the brass bands. Also very visible is Paignton Pier with a portion missing to make it more difficult for invading forces to get ashore.

A closer view of the break in the Pier with a length of decking and supports removed.

*Opposite above:* Colonel Robert Smith built the Redcliffe Tower which was completed in 1865 and modelled on Indian architecture. It was renamed the Redcliffe Hotel in 1902.

*Opposite below:* The attractive entrance hallway is typical of the Edwardian period.

Paignton, Hotel Redcliffe

These two ladies epitomise the relaxing pleasure of sitting on Paignton beach.

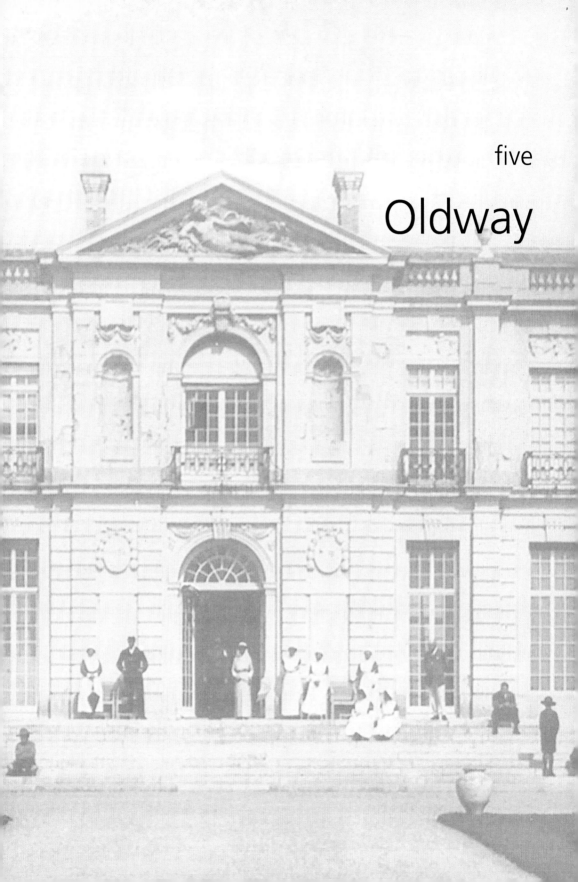

five

# Oldway

Oldway Mansion was built for Isaac Merritt Singer who produced a working sewing machine which could be manufactured in great numbers. Sadly he died in 1873 before the building was completed.

*Opposite above:* During the First World War Isaac Merritt Singer's son, Paris Singer, allowed the building to be used as an American Women's War Relief Hospital. It was visited by Queen Mary, wife of King George V in September 1914. She is standing on the steps of Oldway in the centre of the group. On the far right is the matron in her nursing uniform.

*Opposite below:* The wounded were looked after by 151 staff including sixteen American sisters, three of whom were male, twenty-one probationers and eight surgeons when the Somme offensive began in 1916.

Matron, standing in the doorway, is flanked by seventeen nurses, a few senior staff and some of the 'Patrol of Boy Scouts' who gave assistance as volunteer stretcher bearers. This carefully posed photograph was taken on the same day as the royal visit.

On 27 September 1914, the first war wounded arrived at Paignton station from Southampton watched by a large cheering and waving crowd. The servicemen were driven in GWR buses and ambulances to the hospital at Oldway Mansion.

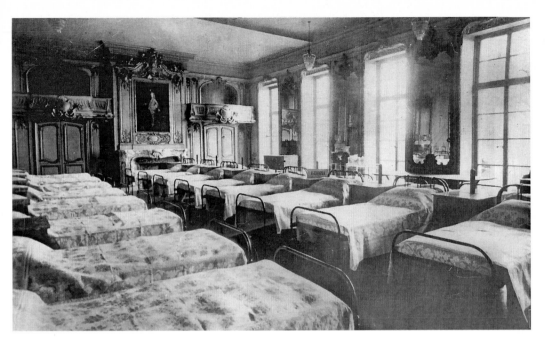

The Alexandra ward in the mansion's ballroom waiting for the arrival of the injured servicemen. The beds are fully prepared and by 1915 there were as many as 255 patients who had an average stay of thirty-one and a half days.

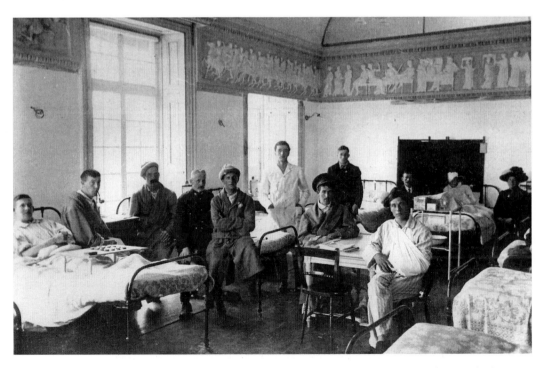

Some of the wounded being visited in another room. By 1916 there had only been thirteen deaths out of 3,203 cases admitted. During the influenza outbreak in 1918 about 100 soldiers died.

From 1929 to 1945 part of the Oldway Mansion building and grounds were leased to the Torbay Country Club. In the grounds were two bowling greens with a pavilion, fifteen tennis courts, and also two squash courts which were constructed in the Rotunda.

After a round of golf or a fiercely fought tennis match what better way to unwind than to take afternoon tea on the lawn.

# six

# Town Centre

The Triangle is where Victoria Street, Totnes Road and Palace Avenue converge. Paignton's first place to see moving pictures was at the Picture Theatre which was established in April 1911 when the Electric Palace opened at the bottom of Totnes Road. A flag advertising its presence flies from the top of the building. It is known by many as the Bug House.

*Opposite above:* Oliver Heaviside, a forebear of the author, was best known by the public for his prediction that radio waves were reflected from a layer of ionised gas in the upper atmosphere – the Heaviside Layer. He published many scientific papers on electromagnetism and established a worldwide reputation among scientists and physicists.

*Opposite below:* Oliver moved with his parents from London, where the majority of his most significant scientific papers and books were published. He was thirty-nine years old and lived in Palace Avenue above his brother's music shop where he continued his studies. You can see the 'Pianos for Hire' sign above the shop. It is opposite what is now Rossiter's store.

TORBAY CIVIC SOCIETY

OLIVER HEAVISIDE F.R.S.
1850-1925

MATHEMATICIAN AND SCIENTIST
RENOWNED WORLDWIDE FOR HIS
CONTRIBUTION TO ELECTROMAGNETIC
THEORY AND PREDICTION OF THE
HEAVISIDE LAYER OFF WHICH
RADIO SIGNALS ARE REFLECTED

LIVED HERE
1889-1897

*Right:* Oliver can be seen leaning against a pillar wearing a cap and is behind all the other family members. He suffered all of his life from varying degrees of deafness so did not socialise very well. A keen pedal cyclist, he had probably cycled there on his own.

*Below:* Plagued by jaundice and other ailments all his life, he finally succumbed to prostate cancer and died in 1925. He was buried at Paignton Cemetery in a family grave shared by his parents. His name was added to their headstone.

*Opposite above:* This plaque was recently put up on the site of the former music shop (now part of Barclays Bank) where Oliver and his parents lived. From left to right: Ena Hocking, deputy mayor David Buckpitt, mayor Heather Buckpitt, the author, Jeanne Heather and Ian Handford.

*Opposite below:* To celebrate his father's eightieth birthday the Heavisides went by horse and carriage on a family outing to Berry Pomeroy Castle, halfway between Paignton and Totnes.

Winter and clearly a busier time of day.

*Opposite above:* Looking up Palace Avenue around 1895 you can just see the Heaviside music shop sign on the left and Dellers Stores on the right.

*Opposite below:* Taken around 1890, the building on the corner has yet to be occupied and the space above is for a town clock which awaits installation.

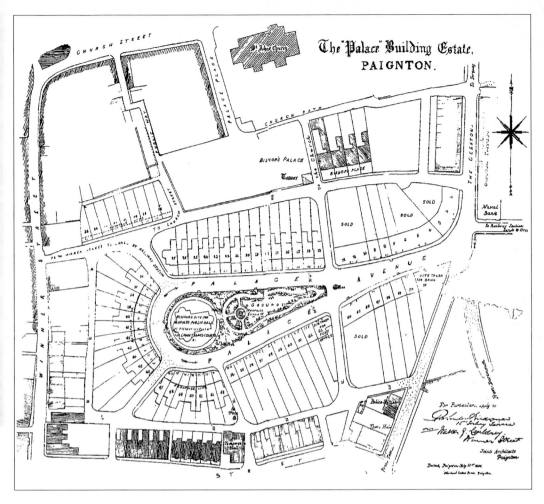

Architects Bridgman & Couldrey's joint plan for the design of Palace Avenue and its gardens dated and signed on 21 July 1886.

*Opposite above:* Looking down from Palace Avenue gardens at the previous scene, and towards the junction with the Torquay, Totnes and Dartmouth Roads.

*Opposite below:* Palace Avenue Gardens with its well-remembered monkey-puzzle tree, the big tree and the Wesleyan church. The houses on the right were all turned into shops.

Isambard Kingdom Brunel was a brilliant engineer and inventor who built great ships and bridges as well as the Great Western Railway. He died in 1859 at the early age of fifty-three. He was always kind and considerate to all his employees no matter how low their status.

*Opposite above:* Brunel bought land near Bishop's Tower (later Coverdale Tower) from the local parish and in 1857 built four houses for his senior staff who he wanted to ensure worked in the very best environment. No. 1 Bishops Place was for the company doctor with space at the rear to house a coachman with a stable so that he could do his calls, No. 2 housed Brunel's architect/surveyor, No. 3 was allocated to the chief engineer and No. 4 to the chief procurer (buyer).

*Opposite below:* Bishop's Tower (later Coverdale Tower) and the surgery built for his doctor across in Bishop's Place has remained in medical occupation for over 150 years and today is still a busy doctor's practice. Brunel's sojourn in Paignton is being officially recognised at the refurbished surgery where large open fireplaces, tiled floors and other features that were part of his design are being preserved.

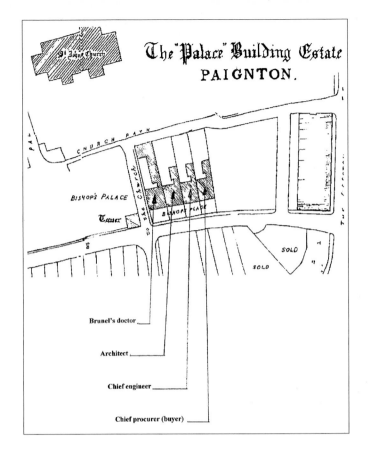

The "Palace" Building Estate
PAIGNTON.

St John's Church

CHURCH PATH

BISHOP'S PALACE

Tower

BISHOPS PLACE

SOLD

SOLD

Brunel's doctor

Architect

Chief engineer

Chief procurer (buyer)

Paignton, Old Tower.

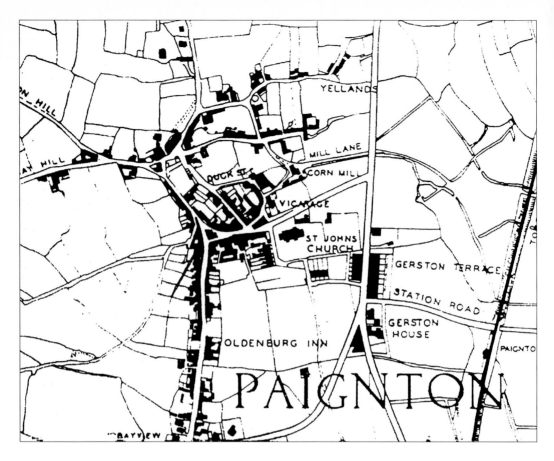

*Above:* The 1863 map shows the town when Winner Street was the main shopping street and housed the Oldenburg Inn which was the main hotel in the town. The railway station is still depicted as on the marshes; the fields behind the Oldenburg later became Palace Avenue and its gardens. Duck Street is now named Princes Street.

*Left:* A very rare photograph of Shepherd's Oldenburg Hotel with Mr John Shepherd standing in the doorway under the entrance columns with his young son Archie. It is now the Oldenburg Inn.

*Right:* In 1902 there was a very serious fire in Winner Street just beyond the Globe Inn which made ten people homeless. This was the picture printed in the press at the time.

*Below:* Victoria Park was completed at the end of 1894 after the marshy ground had been compulsory purchased by the council from the Dendy Trustees. When the pond was finished at the end of 1895 the council was given a swan to put there.

The park was designed by architect George Sowdon seen here sitting alongside the stream near where Paignton Library now stands. Behind him is his home in Courtland Road.

In the 1950s the original swan's descendants appear to have multiplied!

A busy day on Torbay Road. A GWR motor bus, creating plenty of smoke from its exhaust, is making its way to the seafront. On the right is the famous Cycling Tourist Club (CTC) emblem showing where cyclists can stay.

Torbay Road, *c.* 1908. Deller's Café is on the right and further down there is a space where a new prestigious Deller's Café is to be built. Also on the right is a branch of Iredales Library which published the earliest street maps of Torbay.

The new café is still under construction in 1910 by local firm of builders, C. & R. Drew.

*Above:* Opened in 1911, Deller's Café was described as a 'building of outstanding architectural merit and beauty'. It had been designed by architects Messrs Hyams & Hobgen on the instruction of Mr William Lambshead who already owned Deller's supply stores in Palace Avenue.

*Right:* The ornate and well-loved entrance to the new Deller's Café is one of which many people today still have fond memories. Not only for the café but for its ballroom which was the scene of many great social occasions.

An interior view of the café which looks onto the tea garden.

A view of the tea garden.

To the great regret of Paigntonians the building was demolished in 1965.

Cabbies outside the Gerston Hotel waiting for fares, *c.* 1897. By 1912 their fares were: drawn by one horse or two ponies or mules – one hour or less 3s. Horses were well catered for with a nearby water trough.

In 1912 when the motor bus and the horse-drawn cabs were competing for custom.

A lot is going on in this view. Note the police box in the centre and the poles carrying telephone lines above the shops on the left-hand side of the street.

Familiar to perhaps only a few people nowadays, this scene shows the layout of the old level crossing and iron bridge.

The very busy Torbay Road.

Rough sea, Preston.

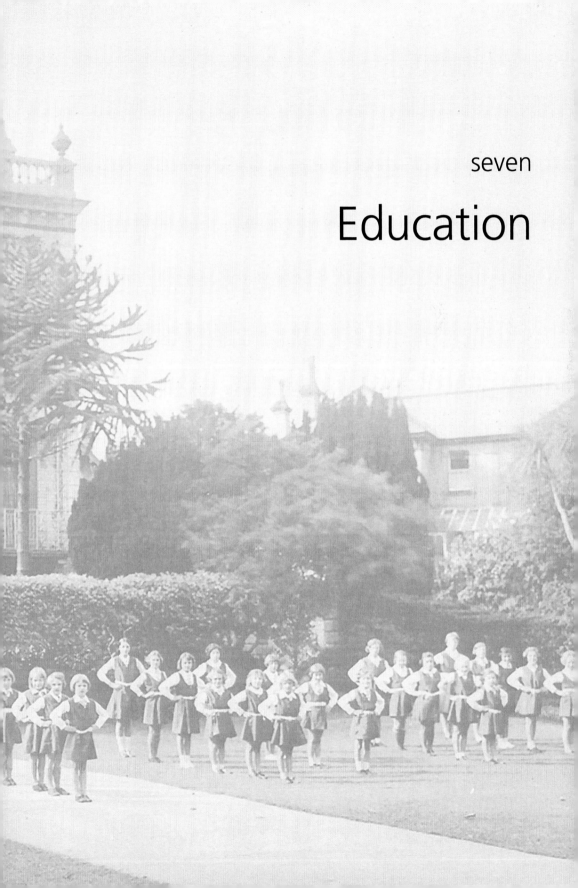

# seven

# Education

In 1908 the Marist Sisters, a group of Catholic nuns, bought Tower House in Fisher Street. They made it into a school for girls, which was very popular and enlarged in 1930. Their most famous pupil was Sue Barker, tennis player and sports television presenter. Tower House School took over the old Marist Convent when it was closed in 1982.

Many former pupils will remember Our Lady's Grotto at a side entrance to the school.

Junior Forms in front of Convent.

Over fifty junior girls posing for the school photographer who is probably using a long exposure time with his camera. One can only wonder whether keeping all those girls so still could happen today. There is no teacher in sight.

Senior Forms in front of Convent.

The senior forms are behaving themselves with equal precision. The author wonders whether the nuns made them keep their hands on their hips to prevent them from waving their arms around.

Paignton School in 1906. It was located in Hyde Road and later run on Grammar School lines as Paignton College. Desks are supported by metal work similar to a sewing-machine frame and have a seat on the front to allow another row to be added. It closed in the 1930s and became the Croft Hotel which was later demolished to make way for the Crossways shopping complex.

eight

# Entertainment

Sand sculptor David Anning was a well-known sight in the 1920s and 1930s on local beaches. This is his Androclese and the Lion sculpture. Androclese was a first-century Roman slave who fled from a cruel master to the African desert. Whilst there, he removed a thorn from the paw of a crippled lion. Recaptured and sentenced to combat a lion in the arena he found his adversary was the same lion. Roman emperor Tiberius freed them both.

The Lyrics singing group performed through the summer weeks from various places in Paignton and were very popular. Older readers will probably remember them.

*Opposite above:* This appears to be an Empire Day (May 24) production by a local operatic and dramatic society. A lot of interest in the picture but where is it taken? The author would be grateful to hear from any reader who knows.

*Opposite below:* Charles Shadwell was notable for being the conductor of the BBC Variety Orchestra from 1936 to 1967 and was heard regularly on the radio. He was still actively involved with his orchestra at the time of his death at the age of eighty-one in 1979. He is seen here performing at the Summer Pavilion which was demolished in 1965 to make way for the Festival Theatre.

*Charles Stadwell* and His Orchestra, Paignton, 1954

These are members of the Paignton Male Voice Choir. Percy Pearce was their conductor but who are the people in the picture and in what year this image was taken? Perhaps a reader will know.

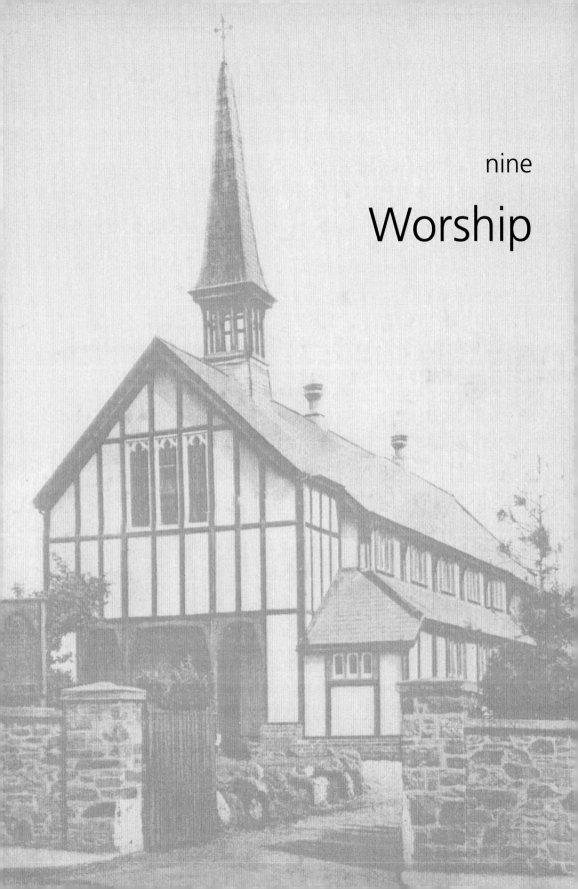

nine

# Worship

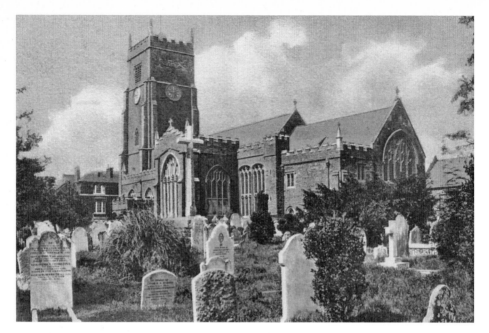

The Parish church shown here around 1890 has changed little in over 100 years. It is the third to be built on the site. Saxons occupied Devon in the eighth century and the first Christian church was probably built soon after. The second church was built by the Normans in about 1100 and foundations of this edifice have been occasionally uncovered.

These sheep in 1907 may be on their way to the slaughter house in Crown and Anchor Way. The Church Hall behind the lychgate existed in 1829 with two rooms for boys and girls and was a National School. It was enlarged in 1846 by adding a room for infants and a house for the teacher. It eventually became the Church Hall and was later incorporated with the adjacent Paignton hospital. A new Church Hall was built near the vicarage in the grounds of the old Bishop's Palace.

The Parish church of St John the Baptist, *c*. 1905. Between 1873 and 1885 much restoration work was carried out: galleries were removed before new pews, several stained-glass windows and a new organ were installed. The cost was met mainly by public subscription and Paris Singer presented the new organ.

A later view showing the new rood screen and behind it you can just see the reredos at the back of the altar. The gift of a new reredos was made by the Chopin Family Association of Maine, USA in 1927. Samuel Chopin, who worshipped there, emigrated from Paignton to America in 1638.

*Left:* The Coverdale Tower as viewed from inside the parish garden. Almost all the views of this landmark have been photographed from outside. Miles Coverdale became Bishop of Exeter in 1553 when he was over sixty years of age. The condition of the roads were very bad and it is unlikely that he ever saw Paignton. That he translated the Bible is believed to be pure fiction.

*Below:* The Baptist church at Preston. The Baptists in Paignton started at the Baptist chapel in Winner Street on land bought for £200 by Miss A.M. Tozer. This Preston church has been greatly enlarged and extended since the Second World War.

*Right:* This is the first St Paul's church in Torquay Road, Preston. The church was dedicated in 1912 and celebrated its Silver Jubilee in 1937. Today's church was consecrated by Bishop Curzon in December 1939.

*Below:* St Andrew's church in Sands Road dates from 1875. The first church was known as the Iron church and the present church, shown here, was erected between 1893 and 1897. It was built using local red sandstone in a fourteenth-century Gothic style. Internally there are Hamhill stone dressings and there is a marble mosaic on the chancel floor. In 1930 it was fully completed when the new west end was added.

*Collaton Church, Paignton*

Collaton St Mary (formerly Collaton Kirkham) was separated from Paignton parish and became an ecclesiastical parish in its own right in 1864. The church was built over the next two years. Washington Singer later gave the land needed for Parish Rooms which were built in 1912.

Mr W. Whitley presented the clock and four bells in memory of four friends who died in the First World War. The parish is now linked to that of Stoke Gabriel.

ten

# Surrounding Places

Marldon on a lovely summer afternoon. On the right is the Church House Inn and up Church Hill on the left can be seen the old school with children (not very clearly defined) in the playground. Further up are the almshouses and above them, on Ipplepen Road, is the now defunct United Reformed chapel.

*Opposite above:* This is the junction with Church Hill and on the immediate left is where Marldon Council built the first of its village halls – a wooden one.

*Opposite below:* The post office was across from the inn. There are now no steps but the door can still be seen on the side of what is now a private house. The Church House Inn reputedly housed the builders of the church. The adjoining old bakehouse is now part of the inn and has been converted into a restaurant; you can see there the old ovens restored and preserved for posterity.

Post Office Corner, Marldon

Compton Castle is not really a castle but a fortified manor house. It was lovingly restored by Commander Raleigh Gilbert some years ago. It is owned by the National Trust and the Gilbert family still live there.

The tidal dam at the mill pond at Stoke Gabriel around 1860.

The church, which is dedicated to St Gabriel, still has its thirteenth-century west tower, the remainder being fifteenth century. The first vicar was Clement de Langford in 1283 when it was then Stoke St Gabriel.

Outside, the churchyard has fine views over the mill pond and the river Dart. It has numerous gravestones including one commemorating George Jackson Churchward, the famous railway engineer. However, its chief glory is a yew tree probably about 800 years old, and possibly older. A traditional rhyme claims to provide a way in which wishes can be fulfilled, 'Walk ye backward round about me, seven times round for all to see; stumble not and then for certain, one true wish will come to thee'.

The Church House Inn and Church Walk. To the right beyond the inn is the old National School built in 1876. It is still used today as a pre-school nursery and for other community activities. Just round the corner on the right and out of view is the Snug bar which the locals use and was, and perhaps still is, the place to hear the real Devon dialect.

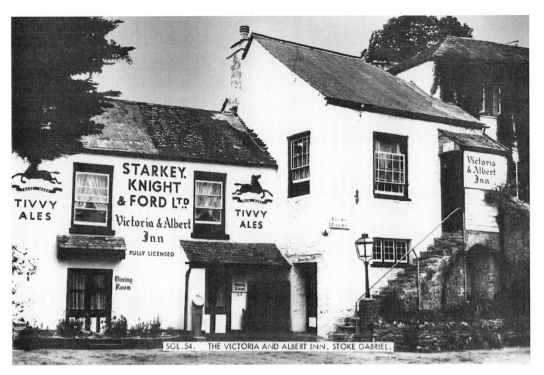

The very popular Victoria & Albert Inn is down the hill in Coombe Shute, a family pub accepting children unlike the Church House Inn in Church Walk.

The thatched cottages at Waddeton Cross on the old road between Paignton and Galmpton. Waddeton House, nearby, is an early nineteenth-century house rebuilt in the Elizabethan style and adjacent to the ruins of an earlier house. In June 1992 it was bought by a 'greetings card magnate'.

*Above:* The Manor Inn, Galmpton. There were a number of different pubs in the area and seeing a coach and horses at the inn would not have been an uncommon site.

*Left:* The author imagines this family have walked from Brixham and their father is asking the postman which road they should take.

Churston Golf Club which was destroyed by fire and replaced by the present modern building. This 18-hole golf course was opened in 1890 on land made available by Lord Churston.

Further on the way towards Brixham is the small historic village of Churston Ferrers which leads to Churston church and Churston Court.

Old Churston Court Inn was originally a Saxon manor where the Saxon Earl Ulf and his son lived. They ruled over all the surrounding land in the first half of the fifth century. After the conquest it was taken over by the order of the Monks of Totnes, so becoming a monastery. It is now Grade I Listed with a fine restaurant and full of history.

Just beyond the boundary of Paignton on the way to Totnes lies the tiny hamlet of Longcombe where a fox hunt is about to take place.

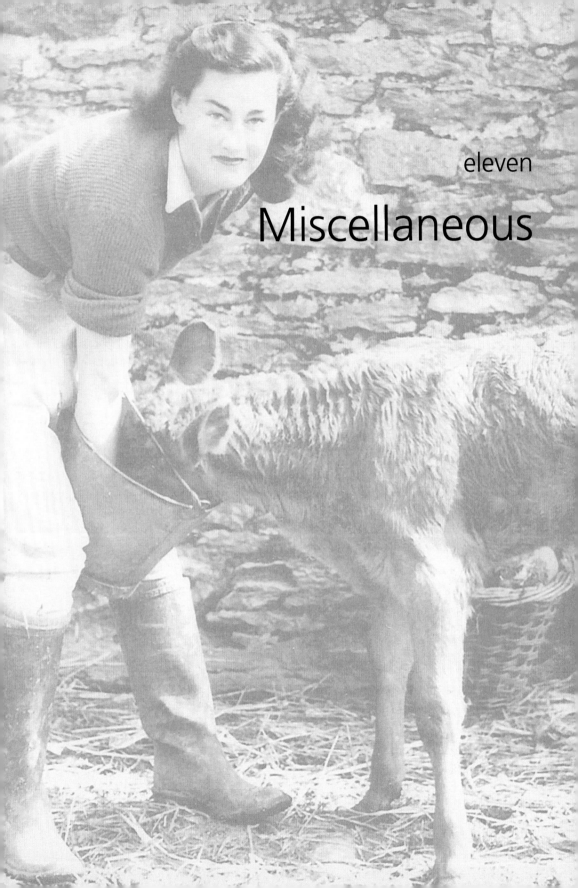

eleven

# Miscellaneous

Marygwen leading the Women's Land Army in the Victory Parade held in Palace Avenue wearing their green jerseys, brown corduroy breeches and brown felt hats.

*Opposite above:* In the Second World War 30,000 men previously working in agriculture had joined the fighting forces so many women volunteers joined the Women's Land Army to work on the land. Marygwen Furneaux was one of them seen here at Longcombe farm feeding a young calf.

*Opposite below:* Marygwen doing a job which the men would normally have done. The women worked very hard doing a wide range of jobs and for long hours. Without their efforts Britain would have been without enough food to survive.

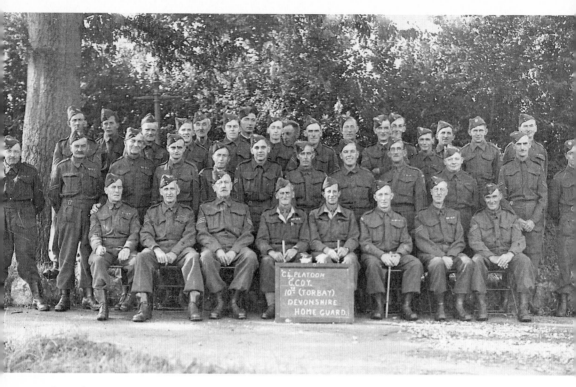

Also replacing men who had been drafted for war service were the Home Guard. This is the local platoon, *c.* 1940.

*Opposite above:* When Herbert Whitley opened his zoo it was also a circus providing entertainment. The council insisted that he paid entertainment tax but he claimed it was purely an educational establishment so while ensuing court cases took place over several years the zoo was closed. Eventually he gave in and the zoo opened again.

*Opposite below:* These chimps are certainly enjoying their tea party in the zoo and sojourn in Paignton. The author hopes you have also enjoyed your visit through the pages of this book.

# Devon's Zoo and Circus

## Primley Zoological and Botanical Gardens,
### PAIGNTON

# Other local titles published by The History Press

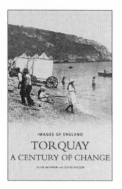

## Torquay  A Century of Change

DAVID MASON AND ALAN HEATHER

Beginning more than 140 years ago, this book explores the style and grandeur of the town, the many fine villas and grand hotels built to accommodate the needs of guests, the evolution of the railway and small villages surrounding the town, the seafront, the shops and traders, and the social occasions and café life of the 1920s and '30s. These images, many of which are published here for the first time, represent a vital part of the town's heritage.

978 0 7524 3960 0

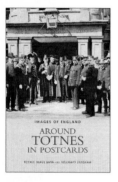

## Around Totnes in Postcards

TOTNES IMAGE BANK AND ROSEMARY DENSHAM

With over 200 archive images and informative captions, this fascinating book takes a nostalgic trip down memory lane. Including postcards from the last century from the Totnes Image Bank, it reveals the people and street scenes of bygone Totnes and the surrounding area. It will reawaken memories for some and offer a glimpse into the past for others, and is sure to appeal to residents and visitors alike.

978 0 7524 3190 1

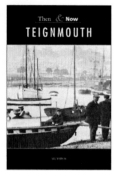

## Teignmouth  Then & Now

VIV WILSON

Teignmouth has seen many changes during its long history as a port, a fishing and boat-building town and a holiday resort. This book illustrates some of the changes that have occurred over the last hundred years by comparing a series of old photographs with modern ones taken from exactly the same locations. The reader can follow the changes and then revisit the locations to see them in a new light.

978 0 7524 3368 4

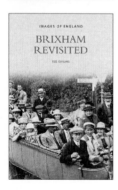

## Brixham Revisited

TED GOSLING

This absorbing collection of images provides a nostalgic glimpse into the history of Brixham on the south Devon coast during the last century. Illustrated with over 200 postcards, this selection recalls Brixham in the heyday of its fishing past. From glimpses of shipbuilding, including the construction of the Mayflower II in 1957, to vistas of the old town streets and buildings, all aspects of working and social life are chronicled here.

978 0 7524 3620 3

If you are interested in purchasing other books published by The History Press or in case you have difficulty finding any of our books in your local bookshop, you can also place orders directly through our website

**www.thehistorypress.co.uk**